A Hint of Eden

Also by Paul Williamson
Ties to Red Hill
Edge of Southern Bright
To the Spice Islands
Moments from Red Hill
The DNA Bookshelf

Paul Williamson

A Hint of Eden

Acknowledgements

Poems in this volume have been published in *Quadrant*, *Cordite*, *Wild*, *I Protest*, *Polestar*, *Tamba*, *Short and Twisted*, *Melaleuca*, *Positive Words*, *Sacred and Profane* and *Blue Nib*.

Thanks to family and friends for support and the shared experiences from which I drew. I am grateful to Les Murray for his support of my poetry and his comments. Thanks are due to Les Wicks for a poetry edit.

A Hint of Eden
ISBN 978 1 76109 196 4
Copyright © text Paul Williamson 2021
Cover image: Janet Sweeney – Murray River, Corowa, NSW

First published 2021 by
GINNINDERRA PRESS
PO Box 3461 Port Adelaide 5015
www.ginninderrapress.com.au

Contents

Beginnings
- A Hint of Eden — 11
- Chances — 12
- Golden Surge — 13
- Feeding the Fevered — 14
- Safe Harbour — 15
- Ned Kelly by Nolan — 16
- Ground Cover — 17
- Chemical Skies — 18
- Edge of the Snowy — 19
- On Anzac Day — 20
- Airport Dawn — 21
- Red Hill Calm — 22
- Connecting — 23
- New Year Walk on Phillip Island — 24
- Tiling the Mosaic — 25

On City Streets
- Early Build — 29
- New Births — 30
- Cherry Blossoms — 31
- Pre-Christmas Mass — 32
- Op Shop Story — 33
- The Café at the Gaol — 34
- Reclaiming the Square — 35
- Rainbow in Brunswick — 36
- Neighbourhood Park — 37
- Dies Irae — 38
- Return Network — 39
- Royal Hospital — 40

Robust Friends	41
Rose Street Markets	42

Along the Way

Woolshed Wedding	45
Small Town Near the Highway	47
Stone Knife	48
Revelations	49
Bushfire Refugees	50
The Rains Come	51
Gasoline Way	52
Hard Plains	53
Northern Day Trip	54
At Norfolk Island	55
Clearer View	56
Ocean Swim	57
The Feel of the Sea	58
Viking Blood	59
Another sunset but blazing	60

People on the Journey

Seafaring Father	63
Sandwiches	64
Snapshots of Dad	65
The Family Motto	67
Cogs	68
Wildish West	69
Staging Post	70
Sandstone Steps	71
The Teacher	72
Laundry Love	73
The New Grandchild	74
The Pan Child	75

Leaving the City	76
Down the Hill	77
Time Out	79

Breezes in the Trees

Spirit of the Land	83
Belonging to this Place	84
Staying Close	85
Autumn at the Arboretum	87
From the Tree	88
Stages	89
Shipwreck Garden	90
Chinese New Year	91
People of the Hill	92

The Circle

Winter Break	95
Next Stage	97
A Coming	98
Cutting in	99
Mandala	100
Easter Change	101
Blessing	102
Return	103

Beginnings

A Hint of Eden

At the coastal edge south of Batemans Bay
humpback whales feed and breech in springtime
as fishing fleets work cobalt depths
filling stores and markets with technicolour catches
and oyster farms stretch on light turquoise
near mangrove flats and sandy bays.
In summer, storms send racing yachts limping to port
and grind beaches from rock faces.

Onshore below the misty escarpment clothed with bush
near Moruya, Bodalla, Narooma and Bermagui
dairy herds gift cream for cheese
beef cattle fatten, sheep give wool
log-laden trucks rattle the highway
artists work and diversely create
hippies sell in startling colour
retirees and Centrelink customers settle seaside
as tourism firms the towns.

The Yuin Nation Salt Water people remain
but not now in cool-fired hunting landscapes.
Now summer brings hot blazes to eucalypts
crowded by casuarinas, vines and wattle.
Yet in the early autumn after the summer tourist frenzy
the coastal strip still conjures thoughts of Eden.

Chances

Revolution in America redirected British convicts
sent them here to start the new colony.
Settlers and merchants came in wind driven hope.
Scottish crofters fled starvation.
Potato famine launched migrants from Ireland.
Fevered American, Chinese and European miners
rushed for gold and built this nation.

More migrants came from the rubble of war in Europe;
some were ten-pound Poms.
Hunger sent farmers from Greece and Italy.
A lost war in Vietnam launched boat people.
Now religious fighting drives the weary from the Middle East.
Opportunity draws the skilled to settle
and families reunite.

Golden Surge

The town grew fast and crowded
on easy nuggets
grasped and cashed for red-brick
merchant buildings, official stone;
shops and homes near mine shafts.

Slab huts close to diggings sheltered new arrivals
as the population surged at Ballarat.
Chinatown with its colourful shops
grew on the margin.
Soldiers were billeted in canvas tents.

A frozen replica of Sovereign Hill
ten years after discovery
shows stores and barn-like saloons
stagecoach and smelting factories
an Anglican Church and a school.

Eureka Stockade the colony's best-known revolt
rests defiant scant kilometres distant.
Lalor and followers resisted a miners' tax
got bloodily put down but changed the law.
Their flag flies now for left and right.

The town still cherishes its fevered start
but mines have mostly gone; panning creeks are quiet
as other work supports the hundred thousand.
In a shop window the replica Golden Hand nugget
shines a foot long and half as wide.

Feeding the Fevered

Along the Moyne River from Port Fairy
that survived on the toil of sealers and whalers
immigrants lured from Belfast found
new lives as tenant farmers
growing crops to feed the goldfields.

The farmland seemed like Ireland
lush green from volcanic soil
basalt for loose rock fences around fields
as tenants swapped one testing life for another.
Headstones tell how many children died.

The Southern Ocean's roaring forties
like the Atlantic of home
helped farmers keep connections
until the Shipwreck Coast sank two of three ships
from the Belfast line, and mostly cut ties;

yet roads still have names
like Reardon Street and McGill Circuit;
Belfast scribed on town signs.

Safe Harbour

Port Bridgewater Bay was Portland's safe port
for early merchant ships, sealing boats and whalers
risking the Shipwreck Coast
before those industries faded.

The thriving colonial port town
is replaced by a corrugated-iron boatshed
slowly eaten by salty rust
while it waits out winter for summer tourists.

Around and under the iron-meshed wooden jetty
five young Australian fur seals swim in their nursery;
healthy, active, sleek, whiskered
sometimes stopping to squabble with siblings and playmates

or to watch the watchers.
There are treats on offer sometimes.
Nearby adults non-murderously bite each other's necks
or sit on sea-worn basalt rocks to scratch.

Offshore near purple shadows of submerged kelp
an Australian gannet plummets into turquoise, close to the seals
safe here from sharp teeth and the pounding Southern Ocean.

Ned Kelly by Nolan

His head space is like the harsh climate
lightning flashing between clouds in seared sky.

Irish in origin with British overlords
from five centuries of invasion

now on a stage of tortured yellow not green
struggling grasses, struggling trees, harried farmers

the musket-bearing rider from convict stock
black clothes, iron helmet, is for the troopers

a window on death's land, where much that lives
is deadly when hunted to a corner

where much that lives kills or is killed.
Such is life.

Ground Cover

The first fleet carried rabbits for food
but they took the land. They fed and burrowed
across the country. Some meat was taken
and fur was pressed into Akubra hats.
Grandfather trapped them for food in the Depression
near the Parramatta river as a factory nightwatchman;
Rabbitos caught coneys to sell on the streets.

Below the brow of the grassy climb
descendants from those plagues
scamper with fluffy tails, nursery fur.
They survived myxomatosis and calicivirus
launched to destroy them
as they stripped the hopes of graziers and farmers.

Now as I walk on grass beside this Townsville beach
in the heat of sugarcane country
cane toads, a later introduced pestilence
move the ground under my feet
waiting for somehow to stop their spread.

Chemical Skies

Smoke-filled air is flecked with dead embers.
Orange monk-robe skies paint dusk
in day. Birds roost for the scorching night.
Chemical wind barges
roars heated threats.
The fiery wall hits the house
searing shudders rattle doors
air vents blast from the roof
burning embers shoot through cracks
filling the rooms. Small fires
inside are quickly doused
so they don't grow to burn.
The front hunts onward
attacks more Canberra homes more lives.
It has happened again; again.

Edge of the Snowy

Eucalypt forests grade south of Canberra into sparse trees
like ancient Ngunnawal or Ngarigo hunting landscapes.
From Michelago to Bredbo green tinged fields
morph into pastel buff-yellow and then the pink and purple
of brutal drought. Cattle and sheep graze on what looks like dirt
or feed the farmers unload. Dams are almost empty.
Cooma lies in the rain shadow where mountains rob clouds.
Gnarled hard-trained pine trees line the roads
of the early town of sandstone and red brick.
The town spreads with buildings of their times.

Snowy Hydroelectric offices testify to immigrants
who left the wreckage of war in Europe for Kosciusko
Jindabyne and Eucumbene to build
the Snowy River Scheme and remain.
Now cars pass to and from changeovers at mountain ski resorts.
The town gleans the pulsing trade.
Police stop drivers to check enthusiasms
of those drawn to fast snow.

On Anzac Day

The crowd streams to where the marchers gather.
Family groups with parents, grandparents and children
line the closed-off main street of Albury.
Distant hills watch from beneath dim haze.
Above them, light straggled clouds cluster
like an ancestral army now at rest.

Beside the highway to Gundagai
a tractor waits to cross from yellow grass to yellow grass.
Sun shines the olive leaves of eucalypts beside the road
far from the war turning attack on Villers Bretonneux
during last night a hundred years ago
fighting for Britain; far from snipers on the Kokoda trail
and from Afghanistan, fighting for Uncle Sam.

We don't hold life cheap or accept our troops will die.
We send our best but want them home safe.

Airport Dawn

Feeling is opaque in the glass
walled Canberra terminal.
Close talk is loud;
far sound hidden by white noise.

Holiday peace almost presides
during the two-hour flight delay.
The excuse is heavy air traffic.
As landing time nears, rare anger sparks
perhaps from something in wider life.

Front runners from the plane
reach the greeting gates to dappled joy.
One starts to wander searching for a familiar face
who arrives breathless to carry bags.

Red Hill Calm

Cars park spasmodically along the access road.
From them born-again cyclists rediscover
downhill bends; young women walk their dogs
while talking with mobile phones;
the always-walkers wear roadside tracks smooth.

At the top of the hill the café is darkened and silent.
Hikers file past socially distanced. At the car park
a grandmother pushes a stroller for her daughter.
Patches of lush grass are herbivore mowed.
Trees have drought hardened trunks but green leaves once more.

The line of centurion bottlebrush
that named the hill, sports sparse blooms.
Blue wrens flit between shrubs
while magpies skirmish and carol.
A raven claims a perch in high dieback.

North towards Civic and south in the Woden Valley
trees look compact in seasonal trim.
The sense is greening after the dry and summer smoke.
In spite of virus restrictions the hill is calm.

Connecting

Hunters stalked kangaroos through this Ngunnawal forest
and scanned from the hills for campfire smoke
from clans that moved through valleys towards bogong moths.
Now from houses below people climb
to watch nature, trail bike or clear weeds
left from when sheep and cattle grazed.

A stately long-dead tree crowns the eastern hill
stretching white eucalypt arms towards the sky.
As I trudge towards it, a young man
slowly paces there. He turns and heads down the track
well spoken, asking quietly how I am
to leave the thought he works at the hospital
in the valley below.

Carefully curled on a boulder is a purple
rope with a golden clip. Close to the tree an ornate belt
rests closed on the rock beside a brightly coloured
cloth collar buckled around the spur of a log;
the way Balinese Hindus pray at a sacred tree.

New Year Walk on Phillip Island

The track bends past a house with bursts
of merriment. Bushes have fluff of spider webs.
In a sky with flimsy pink clouds
the moon is torn in half and shadowed.
A walker from the opposite direction, unsure
like me, nods a greeting in passing.
Cicadas rouse their final chorus.
Birds mumble-tweet late calls.

The narrow way to the water
is lined with twisted trunks of dead melaleucas.
On the beach a family heads home
while silver gulls glide into middle distance.
The band of yellow sand on the distant shore
hints there is a future on the mainland.

Tiling the Mosaic

You cook the porridge
iron a shirt
pack a healthy lunch
work a project
pay bills
mow the lawn
sweep the path
weed the garden
paint a door
take a walk
go to church
meditate a while
have Sunday lunch with family
play with the kids
go on holidays
get flowers for Valentine's Day
not doing that much
just building a life.

On City Streets

Early Build

A sweeping branch of a Moreton Bay fig
hides part of a Hawkesbury sandstone gateway
painted over by city grime
in this former outer, now inner, suburb.

Time-worn blocks show pick marks
without the broad arrow emblems
that claim the convict build
of much of early Sydney.

The stone fence has been removed
around the boundary of the park
now traced with mature trees.
Within roses formalise flower beds.

Children scamper the asphalt path
towards the playground equipment.
Vagrant ibises search for scraps on the lawn.

New Births

The house my parents owned still exists
but entombed among headstone factories
in different myths and thicker car exhaust.
Bandicoots would dig the front lawn
of that post-war fibro house on Sydney's edge.
Tiger snakes used to glide over the wooden fences
while horses grazed the paddocks across the road.

Fathers of friends would file from the bus
with brown paper bottles after six o'clock closing.
On weekends they smoked and watered lawns over beer stomachs.
Our own father had too many children to smoke or drink.
He got over that in the army anyway.
Catholic and Protestant kids heckled each other across streets.
The nuns at primary school dressed in habits
but taught us enough to take next steps.
Father Ford was credible; a chaplain on the Kokoda Trail.
On main roads traffic was thin enough to ride bikes
made at home using frames from the rubbish tip.
Corners had small shops that sold lollies;
musk sticks, cobbers and chocolate freckles.

The mangrove swamp beside the river remains
but the paddocks with remnant eucalypt forests
and the new houses, have gone to city outskirts
a long car drive away on busy roads.

Cherry Blossoms

The hotel is hemmed with colourful narrow streets
where bright red sashes hang between lanterns.
Proprietors in lunchtime stores speak English
better than I speak another language.
Passers-by direct me to Paddy's Market
when I ask the way to a Sydney mall.
I seem the unusual Westerner again
as when I travelled in Asia and
earnestly learnt the customs.

Sights and smells in mind streets linger
from bustling Hong Kong with crispy duck
kimchi and chilli meat amid black ice in Seoul
Tokyo with its theatre of tempura
regal waters of Bangkok where breakfast was fruit-filled omelettes
floral Singapore with raw egg on rice porridge
Djakarta sunsets through spice-filled air.
It is fresh spring again – in autumn
light as cherry blossoms.

Pre-Christmas Mass

I get there early and make for the back pew.
This mass is going to be crowded.
The church is filled with chatter
from people bussed from retirement homes.
Talk pervades as more arrive and find their friends.
Families come minutes before the service.
The noise heads to crescendo.

The priest enters and all is quiet
except for bursts from infant runners.
On the communion queue a young mother smiles
like she recognises the man who collects
groceries for Christmas hampers
from well-behaved kids at the school.
Talk surges with farewells and Christmas wishes
as some rise early to leave

and children still play before the Ark.

Op Shop Story

The road ends as a leafy alcove outside our house
but kangaroos jump the fence from the reserve
to graze the lawn. Possums hiss the high tree paths.

Pilgrims in the dark aimed for the hill behind us
to watch New Year fireworks
start anew with bursting colours.

They tested the yard for thoroughfare
bumped the bins as they walked past
found the padlocked garden gate

then clambered over the back fence
leaving an awkward toll in a designer bag;
a fetching top, priced by the family women.

No one claimed the loss in weeks
so it was washed for an op shop drop
to join the other stories

helping to brighten New Year's.

The Café at the Gaol

The path feels dark beside the high stone wall
of Pentridge Gaol that fills city blocks.
Between Gothic towers that witnessed penance
walls are topped with coiled barbed wire.
The clear glass watchtower came later.

A stone arch frames the gate of iron rods
with pointed ends rampant.
Above, stone balls are on pedestals.
Over the road two bleak churches
seem to promise cold comfort.

The once prison at the city edge
became pricey real estate and was sold
to build apartments inside its shell
near where houses spread north along gold trail
Sydney Road, towards the ring road highway.

The stone-block café with glass-walled veranda
hums with Saturday lunchtime talk
and serves purple taro coffee.
Music is mellow except for a track of hard rock.
Is it a favourite or does it evoke the prison?

Reclaiming the Square

A dozen technicolour stalls
hold a mini local festival
to passively claim the square.
Plants and home-made quilts, cakes and jams are sold.
Some stalls have been lured here from markets.

Fencing by developers has closed off half the square
driving out stores like the fish and chip shop
where our young family bought dinner after church;
for a planned multistorey building
big enough to shadow this well used public place.

Government is pro developer
if locals don't get so restless
they might trouble the ballot box.
Constant resistance was met with jibes
'they're crazy greenies'

but reduced the planned building enough
to leave some sunshine in the square.

Rainbow in Brunswick

Granddaughter wants a working lunch
under the sky-blue ceiling
and the children's paintings that hang
like tropical birds aflight.

Walls are bright with collages
as earnest painters work at rustic wooden tables
children share with parents.
Strings of plump beads for makings are sold on site.
A girl from Mothers' group smiles
then calls out a greeting from where she sits
with mother and friends.

Young adults spanning the gender rainbow
serve lunch in café style
with technicolour cakes
to feed the inspiration.

Neighbourhood Park

We walk the park with an active family companion
a curly coated brown truffle hunter; good company.
Another walker's black Staffy chases a ball;
our dog joins the sprint with open energy.
Nearby an escaped cockatiel feeds on seeding grasses.

A distracted Pacific black duck
waddles towards the weed covered water of the creek
that feeds the drying summer pond.
A blue plastic ball is caught in its reeds and mud
soccer-sized but for younger children.

Near a picnic table at the top of the rise
four-year-old children play, girls in pink or mauve dresses
ribbons in hair, boys in good shorts and coloured shirts
waiting for the birthday cake.

Dies Irae

Homes are low and ranch style
dotted among trees
that grow to ten metres distant.
Dead leaves and fallen trunks litter the ground.
The school nearby is single-storey;
the hospital one floor higher.

Gum trees cluster near car parks
around the footy oval
where Magpies play Tigers, girls and boys;
the trees stretch high near pines and shrubs
that colour in calm, bright weather.

Regional firefighter sirens sound a test.
Threats here have been extinguished for decades
so evacuations have been short.
Deadly blazes were further inland
some towns all but lost.

The crowd ignores the spectre
of trees prime for burning.

Return Network

Beside the asphalt road to the drive-in theatre
the block holds a row of dull green stables
under a line of pylons tethered by power lines.
The red-brick house is faded 1940s smart
the barn a monument to a business.
A dingy white horse patrols alone like a ghost.

At the rubbish-strewn end of the road
the freeway rumbles with traffic
masked behind a strip of eucalypts.
That nature corridor and railway verges
have become links on migration pathways
bringing long-nosed bandicoots
and other wildlife back to Sydney.

Royal Hospital

Uniformed paramedics head briskly to their van.
Ambulances, sirens off, flash emergency lights.
A surgeon in blue linen and plastic tie-on hat
hurries back from a break, eating a salad roll.
Nurses walk preoccupied in baggy navy scrubs.

Red-brick and sandstone buildings
repaired for relentless use are tacked to edges
of colleges now painted with city grime.
In the café multicultural staff and the Sydney crowd
don't linger over food.

A woman hurries by on the edge of tears
as a grey-haired woman and adult son head for pilgrimage.
On the footpath smokers pause; most seem young and fit
below walls of public windows
where lights care day and night.

Robust Friends

No scent but coffee pervades
the cafés' cheery chatter
constant, crisp then bursting

until an unconscious deeper breath
unmasks the subtle smell of books
absorbed, comforting.
My eyes scan the airy library foyer

to be slowly drawn outside
across the broad concrete stairs
to trees in autumn turn
mild rust tones and recent yellows

rain-weathered trunks
preserving like the written word.

Rose Street Markets

The Fitzroy art market sells journeys
lit by different moons
guided by different stars
provisioned and prepared for
from a scatter of beginnings.
Paintings in stalls between the urban
brick walls show connections to oceans
nature and cultural fantasies.

Some frame iconic photographs.
Other journeys end as silver smithing
understated and calm
classic oriental decorations
or rock or resin jewellery.
Sellers watch visitors hopefully
and smile confirmed when sales are made.

Along the Way

Woolshed Wedding

The muted silver corrugated-iron shed is ample;
its window rims painted burnt burgundy.
Inside, the spine for the shearers' combs waits
below rafters decked with strings of small white lights.
Structural columns are tree trunks, split or trimmed;
the wooden walls are hung with rusted farming tools
horse regalia, stencils for absent wool bales
newspaper cuttings from two centuries past.
Outside the back wall are weathered grey mustering pens;
nearby, sheep and cattle sparsely graze the fields to the dam
lined with trees and home for ducks and coot.

Mother waits at the shed, while in Braidwood, the bride
and Father pass the butchers shop that shows their surname.
A clydesdale draft-horse-cross nobly draws their shiny
black open carriage with polished lamps and gold trim;
steered with leather harnesses through silver rings.
Buildings the party passes are traditional and well maintained
sandstone or old brick. Clusters have been rendered
and painted subtle colours. Shop fronts dot the highway
from coast to city and glean the passing trade.
Slowly the horse trots along side roads past paddocks
lush from recent rain, towards the congregation

that stands in an arena rimmed by granite boulders and
rusted machines that had plowed and planted, harvested
and bailed hay. On lawn rough from former farming
the unselfconscious crowd, young and old, family and friends
waits wearing cheerful clothes in diverse styles.
Toddlers cling to parents, one mother lingers
metres away from her newborn held by her husband.
The celebrant stands before a long, rusted bench
of former farm machine decked with rustic flowers
that sprout from preserving jars. Ambient pipes of Pan
play to bless the old and new fertility.

Small Town Near the Highway

Born as a Lachlan River crossing and depot
halfway between Yass and Goulburn
before the gold trail to Sydney came
it earned its red brick and rendered buildings
a post office and church; later a garage.
Now sheep graze all around
as the highway shrinks distance.

The memorial of three wars
has a hundred names
as many as homes in the town.
A stretcher bearer from the Great War
became town doctor.
His sturdy memorial bench
is cut from solid eucalypt.

Tourism keeps the town here.
The hamburger at the café
is all good beef.
The deciduous trees nearby
seem like spirits stretching skywards.

Stone Knife

There is movement all the time on the hill.
In daylight hours, wrens flit
galahs search the hollows, kangaroos
spirit between tea tree and eucalypts.

Through moon-washed still nights
under Ngunnawal stars or cloud
boobooks hoot, frogmouths drift, possums
scurry and hiss high springtime.

Father carries his child on his shoulders today.
Mother follows with a spare warm jumper.
A cyclist strains along the rough track
speaks, head turned in passing.

Now on the hard ground of the ancient
hunters' mound, I find the forgotten stone knife
left when the clan moved onward.

Revelations

Travelling in a fog of smoke
from fires burning inland and to the north
we drive at dawn to beat the midday swelter
after two days of record-breaking heat.
A teenager has just berated world leaders
for damaging the earth and its future.

From Yass heading south smoke hides
everything near the highway.
The bridge road out of Gundagai
looks like a passage into the clouds.

Afterwards the nearby smoke thins.
Trees are green and dams half full.
Trucks laden with hay head north
to feed stock in lingering drought.

The weathered wrought iron farm house roof
tells a story of generations.
In a paddock four horsemen wait.
It is hard to make out what is in the distance.

Bushfire Refugees

Escaping threat and loss from coastal fires
the file of vehicles winds away from Bega
along the tree-lined Snowy Highway for Albury.
They arrive too tired to seem relieved.

Driving for Melbourne next day in smoke
trucks dodge the clusters of caravans and cars
some with roofs packed with camping gear and surfboards.
A van with bench seats covered in faded green plaid
soldiers on in the slow lane looking like it had journeyed
to market for the last ten years; twenty kilometres weekly.

Breeching smoke from northern fires
finds clearer sight and breathing
until smoke thickens again from fires to the south
from Gippsland around Walhalla and Lakes Entrance;
there Defence Force ships evacuate
another crowd of bushfire refugees.

The Rains Come

The Lachlan I slept beside as a child is flooding;
Father and I in the back of a ute under bright stars
before a day at work with artesian drillers.

Now El Niño is leaving in a tantrum of rain.
The town of Forbes is under siege;
roads that go near are closed.

Here to the east falcons and kites
sail the wind through sunny breaks
to drop on unseen prey near grazing cattle.
Paddocks are English green.
The normal dusty grey sheep are now cream.

Creeks swirl muddy water tearing away banks
to send clear rills down sodden slopes
where frogs croak in long grass
and claim flat land for shallow lakes
that eucalypts seem to wade across.

Caravans, ships of the road, return to home port.
In a paddock a bewildered emu.

Gasoline Way

Sunshine lights the clearing
below the giant mountain ash
that grow beside the road.
Long scarves of tan bark
decorate their smooth grey trunks.
Tree ferns cluster around the feet
along with hardy low grasses.

In the town, cottage gardens
flaunt azalea and agapanthus.
Loud signs shine from shops
that lure the passing trade.
The light-filtered tunnel of the forest road
traps exhaust from cars and trucks;
carbon monoxide among the trees.

Hard Plains

Rough scrub and heat belong to him.
The big red ignores our presence,
he bounds on regally close to the truck
in the rusty desert where we peg survey lines
and turn dark from the sun.
I feel a desert visitor, not a stranger
in this my country.

They say I won't like West Texas
but it conjures up the red desert
hot and dry with low scrub
inside a grid of foreign fences
but deer instead of kangaroos.
We don't work on the first day of hunting season
target an early start the next day.

Northern Day Trip

In desert country, sickness country
demons dance with kangaroos, turtles
on faces of rock laced with minerals
poisoned in heat since the dreamtime.
Sword grasses, recently burnt
frame flat red dust between tufts and rock.
Short eucalypts carpet to the straight horizon.
Little corellas spruik mischievous mobs.
Brolgas and jabirus feed on floating grass fields
as magpie geese crowd edges of mud
near flows of eels and barramundi;
indigent crocodiles sponge the end of the wet.
Spirits of distant smoke
mark the hunters' search for life
while whistling kites patrol cinders
seizing shadows of struggle.
Among the trees a dingo haunts
as the aged sun in a sky of red ochre
lords over darkening earth
glows in a People's flag.

At Norfolk Island

The bookstore at the convict ruins
tries to ignore its first lodgers
offers glossy books on mutineers
or island views speckled with Norfolk pine.
There is no blood from those early times
but what is in the ground
or seeped into the stones.
Veins in the population
pulsate with nautical tales.
Tropicbirds alone remember first blood
trail red banners in respect.

Clearer View

In the fog of daybreak
the road ahead is lost in mist
until the veil lifts and nearby paddocks
look lush and flat, comfortable for stock.

We reach low hills, that glower
uninviting, bare and barren
while the asphalt winds up rises
to cliffs with jagged edges.

In the last miles the trip is tight
hemmed by stony faces
that make the way tortuous
until the wide shine of playful ocean.

Ocean Swim

Hovering above the underwater field
with its grass of seaweed and a sandy
current carved channel where a toadfish
burrows to watch with only button eyes showing
as a banjo shark passes, then sleek whiting
after a mirror of fingerlings;

here at the boundary of the water world
and the air realm off Phillip Island
where the whiskered tern flies.
I move slowly, snorkel breathing
knowing I only visit here but belong
with the paddle boarders on the rocky outer break
or on the sandy beach with its white line
of cuttlefish bone and dark dried seaweed.

The Feel of the Sea

Across from colourful paintings in the children's studio
past the smell of fresh paint on empty gallery walls
hangs a clear view of George Lances' muse.
Onshore spoke briefly to him but promptings that endured
were from the turning moods of sea and sky
with troubled clouds and scarce rays of light
above crashing waves near sandstone teeth
as ships plied commerce off Warrnambool
during the turn from sail to smoking iron.

The Shipwreck Coast claimed its victims.
The *Free Trader* was storm-wrecked, sails shredded
then torn away, on the shore near the Old Windmill.

George was a musician, technician, writer and artist.
He helped to found this gallery
across the road from the Whalers Hotel.
He had gone to sea and felt it.

Viking Blood

Some here are only happy at sea
joining our company to be organised
and protected from their onshore selves.
Others want to turn for home
the moment they set sail;
both sail well with us
as we survey the Southern Ocean with sound
quizzing the plunging margin
to learn its story.

The crew out of Hobart is Viking blood;
Their red and white ships are far from home
ice strengthened for the Antarctic
taking us to Macquarie Island
where we survey its make-up and birth.
This is part of the crew's summer journey.
The sea calls in their blood.

Another sunset but blazing

purple and orange strips across the west
one narrow, one wide
and in between them blue sky
holds me to the garden seat
to watch the old tribal friend.

Slowly the colours dim and ends darken
shrinking towards a bright spot
at a peak of the Brindabellas
to creep down slope to the east
to dusk on the other side of the ridge.

Sadness falls like I am a child
called from dusk play.
Possum night will hold until bird-call dawn.

People on the Journey

Seafaring Father

Oceans would call and he would follow
to earn the family's bread.
Work was for one or two months
but for the children the absence was long.

After one stint he drove
from a northern port
to the home of his parents
where his wife and children visited.

The little girl opened the door
looked up at him with eyes that said
it looks like Daddy but isn't
not last time – not this time.

After half an hour sitting with daughters
held in his arms
the feel relaxed to nearly normal.

Sandwiches

Grandad died before I was born
killed by a Stuka dive bomber at Tobruk;
Nana never saw his body.

When Dad came home from war
he looked after Grandad's canaries
in the backyard aviary near the side fence
perhaps with some faint hope he lived.

Nana fed homeless men who stopped at her gate.
Many must have been returned soldiers.
She sent my brother or me with sandwiches.
Her house would have been on the circuit
passed on by word of mouth
or chalk marks on footpath or fence
telling where to find the next meal.
Grandad never came.

Snapshots of Dad

At the still point of the turning world, there the dance is. – T.S. Eliot

After leaving high school at fourteen
as a buck-toothed ugly duckling
Dad swots to become an industrial chemist.
> For a birthday present at twenty-one
> he gets his front teeth removed
> for dentures
then he joins the army like his father Harry and brother Jack
for the Second World War;
Harry is killed, bombed at Tobruk.
> Dad marries Ellen who bears their son
> as he rides a Harley
> an East Indies army mechanic.
At war's end he goes to uni
on a Repatriation Scholarship;
a settled Mother gives birth to me;
> my sister comes the night before the final exam;
> he can't take the US uni scholarship
> with the army debt to repay.
Dad becomes a water geologist well-liked in the bush;
takes some of us children to watch gushing water bores;
steak and eggs for breakfast with the drillers.
> After work each day his young wife dresses for him
> in their bank-owned fibro house.
> The family grows.
He gifts my brother and me poetry because we get it
when he reads us The Hound of Heaven;
we both become published writers.

>He prays after Communion and lives in hope;
>gives me God because he has God
>but doesn't talk much about it;

becomes a competition photographer;
wins some equipment;
takes to wood turning in retirement.
>Mum dies of cancer as she does her Arts degree
>after raising ten children.
>Family gathers to her for her last.

At ninety-two Dad dies foetal in sleep.
Family learned from him.

The Family Motto

Mother and Father lived with feeling
from their twenties in a house they would pay off in thirty years.
Nearby paddocks held childhood wonders.

Caning was relentless at school;
Father belted the kids from tradition;
still they taught us enough.

I listened for useful advice
like the cobbled family joke motto
nil bastardo carborundum
        'don't let the bastards wear you down.'

Cogs

A friend's father invented and fixed cars behind his house.
The son of a blacksmith, he shuffled among black-oiled spares
spread on the concrete floor and benches; appraising
eyes and thinning hair, a gap-toothed grin on oil-smeared face.

What he charged to keep my youthful wrecks rolling
changed with how his cash flow fared; on average cheap
sometimes more. The friendly repairer
is buried now. He died of emphysema

like his father; the same lungs, the same smoking.
I used some of his thoughts in gaps through lean years;
and now in later life, for work and sense.

Perhaps my children and grandchildren
now use some cogs from his mind.

Wildish West

Secondary school had classes of seventy.
The headmaster preached rugby league
at the school assembly.

Older, the car behind with lights on high beam
would be the police checking who was driving
the wreck with youthful road-worthiness.

Sergeants held Western Suburbs lads in line
for lesser indiscretions.
They chastised instead of charging.

Rockers with greasy hair and blonde surfies
listened to blaring pub music.
Couples cuddled in cars.

The ballot sent mates to Vietnam
and brought them back
different.

Apprentice training and Whitlam Uni
was done with nightly beer awash
and unemployment under three per cent.

Staging Post

The market bulges with kaleidoscopic wares
at Dandenong on the eastern edge of Melbourne.
Goods greet new immigrants under the wide flat roof
of the time-faded building near small colourful shops
that cluster close to newer supermarkets and parking lots.
An old woman in orange and black national dress
reaches the market door where a statuesque African couple linger.
Muslim women, faces now uncovered, wear head scarves.
Bulky islanders at a table have swapped
warm clothes for T–shirts with shorts in the heat.
A stooped Greek grandmother wears traditional black.
Two old men with middle European faces chat
as an infant sprints down the aisle
towards the fruit and vegetable, meat and fish stalls
near rainbow pastel clothes, toys and cases for cell phones.
Mother follows behind watching carefully.

Expressions are mostly flat like the cloudy day
few smiles and fewer frowns
while many mark time until their next move.

Sandstone Steps

Long and large, sedate in stone
rich in considered history;
the buildings don't alarm.
Paths curve across lawns
through soothing gardens
that students barely see

as they juggle turmoil
from demands of paid work;
the fog of social life and love;
their tension to discern;
and the pains of emerging.

They stretch for higher steps.

The Teacher

Wily eyes smiled as questions spun.
He talked to each as friend.
Grey haired, eating little
he spoke in kindly heresy

openly saying to follow conscience
not laws that demand a march in step;
said no ill word of others;
explained false power plays with logic.

Laundry Love

The woman makes her choice
when he proposes in the laundry
after dating for three weeks.

It feels right to them
but bemuses family
except for his father.

After a windblown drive to the church
with the bearded best man
weary from the long trip to attend
her man risks all for her;
she risks all for him.

The honeymoon is at Wentworth Falls
in the deeply carved Blue Mountains
in a cottage with a soft bed and well-worn furniture.

Each day they walked the tree-lined road to the Falls
to gaze through mist.
They return after years, with grandchildren.

The New Grandchild

The first sight fulfils.
Grandmother says the newborn
looks like her babies at their start;

something about the eyes and head shape;
not the head width – that is from Father.
Do we humans somehow recognise relatives?

I press my face
to the tiny forehead.
That feel of skin is familiar.

The placid one calmly holding
her mother's finger
is surely one of ours.

The Pan Child

The child there I recognise
as the one who woke
when consciousness formed;

at home in long grass paddocks
lightly treed for cover
with wattle, sparse spreading eucalypts

relic quince trees, crab apples;
skylarks, finches
brown snakes and bearded dragons;

blackberry bushes and barbed wire
scattered tadpole ponds
thin reedy grasses growing from the mud.

Blue eyed with curls for hair
scarred below the knees
part of earth's growing realm

eyes with wonder and lasting.

Leaving the City

Young men and women crowd the start.
Touts shout wealth is the prize.
Parents cheer the chance for their children;
hope the race is fair.

Company training is organised
exercises mandated, but wins
come by grinding through stages
set by chance and expedience.

Children and family trap reasons to stay
Ways to survive slowly show.
Gains reap endurance.
After any quiet time

harried tasks await
as life is submerged
and years disappear
honing the craft.

Joy is used up running in a suit
until assignments, living for money
and worry take their wages.
Family and cherished ones seem strangers.

Everyone knows it is sad to leave

Down the Hill

Changing certainties sweep
through crowds who live in bubbles
of artificial importance.
Marketed dreams, reported disasters
steer their minds.
Pundits dole out populist answers
to huntsmen journalists.
Global warming is discussed over drinks
poverty after lunch.

It's the economy stupid;
higher corporate profits
with a rising stock market.
Beware the afflicted
their presence grows expense.
Publicised polluting or deaths
can damage the brand.
Actuaries calculate a human life's value:
it's worth about half a million.
Is it cheaper to advertise reputation
than to spend on safer design?
Accidents might dim the next watch.

Working poor will still labour
when the streets are dormitories.
Let them run to the beat of cash registers.
Keep them tidily hidden, craftily ridden.
Government should care for them.

The hope of a family
drifted through play and school
to work in the city.
Thousands glow like sparks in the big smoke
swirl between buildings
that form shopfronted canyons.
He was swept to the footpath by job loss
beaten down by ill health
to sit invisible
in the shade of a Moreton Bay fig.

From times when death was a septic scratch away
vanities gather dust in museums;
skulls and other symbols of mortality.
Now we live longer than ever
play cards of privilege
often dealt by forebears.
Most manage smoothly enough day to day.
Some buy toys worth months of average wages

as government moans about dole bludgers
and down the hill amid the car exhaust
charity vans feed the ill and homeless.
A chaplain says her gaol holds few bad people.

He sits cross-legged on the street corner
grimy and dazed by misfortune.
His placard asks for money
to help us lift our lives.

Time Out

Lake water ripples.
Pacific black ducks and moorhens delve tails up.
Leaves on the slender gum trees that line the shore
move in summer breeze.

He drifts the cast onto the water
reels it in slightly, watches the ringing float
then shuffles back to the dirt bank.

A jerk on the line disturbs the peace
as a trout snatches the bait
then dives and is reeled to the net.

This hook is removed
returning life to the shallows.
Two will be kept later for the table.

His wife watches from her canvas chair
like the float is a different reality.

Breezes in the Trees

Spirit of the Land

Among the art at Heide the sun-leathered face
wiry, chisel-nosed and bearded with wisdom
watches sharp-eyed for distant rain
to grow the seeding grasses
that feed the wheeling flocks of green parrots.

He comes again with Gippsland showers
face lined with branching streams
that flow to nurture life
in trees and stretching paddocks
under blue skies and red sunsets.

Horned and hawk masked
bringing bad news and better
he wears his fire-blackened coat as kites hunt
through the smoke, yet with green streaks
for sunny days that bring back life.

This is not Sydney Nolan's spirit of the bush
in Ned Kelly's harried settler headspace
but his friend Albert Tucker's
ageless intruder who returns
when the land surges to be reborn.

Belonging to this Place

A dream of Indigenous connection
to billabongs and rivers
hangs installed at the Albury Murray Art Museum;
with images of codfish called Gugabul
jetsam dropped from river gums
reed-caught sticks and branches
moored in the water.

Yorta Yorta and Ngarrindjeri peoples
fed from the Murray larder for millennia
hunting with spears from wooden boats
carved from canoe trees; some still stand
to tell their stories; or trapped
fish with branch and reed nets;
cooked them on small fires on wet reeds in the boats;
summer people clad in short leather aprons
and winter people wearing possum skin cloaks.

Students made items for this art
so Wiradjuri artist Lorraine Connelly-Northey
could form Nginhagu: Belonging to this Place;
using sticks, gum leaves and yellow twine
to conjure what flows from misty morning to sultry dusk
lingering images that morph and recur.

Staying Close

Without sudden movements I walk the track
keeping the kangaroos and magpies near as I pass.
Swallows glide by in hope of insects.
I stop and sit, still and quiet in the forest
watch birds activate among branches
where none seemed there before.
They call back and forth, jostle blossoms and leaves;
thornbills, shrike-thrushes, sometimes honeyeaters.

Groups of Pacific black ducks glide near reeds
as swans navigate the small lake
and wood ducks hold close to grassy banks.
Murray River tortoises have abandoned their sunny-day log
but shapes slowly form out of invisible depths
as they come up to breathe
with only nostrils above the lake water.
When young we fished for them with meat on string
or caught some in fish traps
to keep a few in water troughs in the apple orchard
long necks, hard carapaces, other-worldly.

Under water laden wind at grey noon
we trudge the ruffled wetlands.
Like Christmas tree lights blinking
a mixed flock of small birds
peeps in the dense thicket;
silvereyes and grey fantails, blue and scrub wrens
as crested pigeons cluster on nearby sheltered gravel.
We wade through boot-high grass
holding pace under duress
in a cocoon of stranded peace.

We may have left the life-giving lakes and forests
for houses and towers
but that was in the near past.

Autumn at the Arboretum

Summoned by the imported palate of autumn
we walk the clay path past juveniles
growing into proud stands, showing
successive colour stations on their way to winter.
Other walkers stroll or pause and scan.

Magpies explode in a stream
out of territories jammed in almost harmony
towards the foot of the hill
below where the metal eagle nests.
A dark eagle glides above the pursuers
futile mini magpies, seemingly ignored.

The eagle drops towards the hill to meet
the unseen mate that rises to join
in choreographed flight, drifting onward.

From the Tree

A puzzling pile of grass and sticks
with a suspicion of moving tail feathers
appeared in the crook of a branch
across the road in a tall eucalypt
seen from our kitchen window.

Later, a currawong, wolf black with white flashes
glides from the nearby reserve to the nest
and bends down to feed a chick
that stretches up in dark profile;
long thin neck and slim fig head.

A windstorm drops the chick onto asphalt
to crouch near the fence, pale-mouthed, bedraggled.
Still there next day, it grooms its wings.
Days later, not fully fledged, it flies
to an instant parent for a feed;
an offspring, deceptively durable.

Stages

From a top branch of the tall nest tree
after months of absence
the kestrel hen nervously scans the surrounds.
She eyes me fixedly as I pass.

The magpie hen at the top of the hill
has later concerns. She sits hard on a twig nest
heavy to ward against still freezing nights.
Her mate brings food.

At the base of the rise the doe kangaroo
is finishing the cycle. She grazes
new growth with pouch so large
her joey will soon be her companion.

Shipwreck Garden

The Southern coastal strip claims a hundred-metre width
behind grey beach sand where giant cuttlefish bones
bleach in dark seaweed.
Bushes are short with leathery leaves.
Yellow grass as tough as palm fronds
stretches up from sand near patches of pigface.

Green finches with thick winter feathers look larger
standing proud on tops of scrub for vantage.
A New Holland honeyeater flashes black, white and gold
as it flits between the tight pink flowers on taller shrubs
where tawny crowned honeyeaters also feed.
A little wattlebird flutters to glean insects
while a black-shouldered kite hovers above.

Yet the wind-clipped strip looks somehow formal.

Chinese New Year

Days of rain have festooned paint
on the hill above the capital

completing the display
to cheer the Year of the Tiger.

The trees are costumed in stripes
for a festive parade in tune with China;

jagged yellow, lemon, grey and dark
camouflaged but shining brightly.

The eucalypts have shed their coats
to join the celebrations.

People of the Hill

We walk steadily, without ceremony
towards the sky-crowned crest
while joggers crunch past with smiles behind their eyes
and trail bike riders strain upwards, to trundle
speedily down. All are part of the loose tribe
from hobby groups, offices and homes
that haunts the winding tracks of our hill.

Some come for calm in the cooling breeze
for fitness promised by gritty trails;
to spot native animals, plants and birds
even marking new sightings in notebooks.
Others dig to reverse the spread of weeds
grubbing out feral scrub to bring back native plants;
working with nature to hold our hill.

The Circle

Winter Break

Briefly unencumbered we travel to warmth
on a lazy island in the Keppel Group
close to Yeppoon on the coast near Rockhampton.
Our small boat churns across the turquoise swell.

A heavy rust-encrusted chain waits as mooring
on a beach of white coral pieces, grey pebbles and sand.
Pandanus nuts carpet the ground.
Coconuts drop from trees and sprout warning signs.
Brush thick-knees, the local curlews, stand like statues
outside huts while a sacred kingfisher darts
from a tree to glean insects.
An osprey claims the nearby craggy peak
to scan the ocean for prey as the sea eagle glides.

The eco huts are off the grid but lack little
with small windpower, solar panels, rainwater,
gas for cooking and a nightly log fire near the beach.
Swimmers snorkel blue coral patches
near where small oysters clad underwater rock faces
and polkadot the shallow shoreline.
Others fish the deep pools near rocky points
or paddle-board and kayak to mangroves
the bay protects from summer cyclones.

Woppaburra seafaring people lived here
but were officially removed a hundred years ago.
Now from hills of rust-stained hard sandstone
folded and baked by volcanic plugs
holiday makers watch for humpback whales.
Mercurial weather blows from the Pacific.
Windy then not; cloudy then fine.
Ten degrees warmer than freezing southern home
it's hard to leave this winter.

Next Stage

The harness snaps
then falls away to leave grooves in shoulders
yet the beasts of burden plod
across fields through careless rain
unaccustomed to the new freedom.

Memory holds the strain of the load;
of sustaining hay at end of day.
The years were not cruel
but restrained will and imagination
through the tension of the harness

that became the reason for living.
Gradually our plodding drifts
from the furrow line
into another pattern
until now inconceivable.

A Coming

Who you are is not a mistake
not a mental lapse by providence.
The plan evolved
with complex care to form you
unique, for necessary tasks.
What makes you different
exactly why, is obscure
yet you are called by name and chosen
not to be somebody other than you
but to become most fully you.

Cutting in

Something was expertly taken
while I dozed this Wednesday afternoon
and left me waking different.

An inner scream echoed then dimmed.
Loved ones hovered
while the signs of intruders began to fade.

Something was changed within
works well, holds promise
that was barely there before.

Mandala

He's take-charge, decisive
leaving few words for his wife;
hints of her physical frailty

joking about her occasional gin.
She gives no defence;
'I am like the old Queen Mother.'

Short years later at the shops
he sits without speaking
in the steel-grey wheelchair

pushed by the woman
who remembers the way home.

Easter Change

Homo sapiens emerged unusually clever
perhaps from DNA changes lit by solar flares.
Early cousins faded but left us their genes
as we spread and bred across the earth.

Who could think dry seeds would grow green shoots
or a crawling caterpillar
would be set free as a butterfly
if we had not seen those wonders?

History says the Christ lived two thousand years ago;
a Jewish hill country prophet, who called
us His Body, one with him, preached
love for others and was killed by worldly powers.

To understand the One, Pope Francis says
we should observe the earth around us.
What if the Bible teachings are true
the Son of Man returned to the Father

and lives in all not fully lost?
Surely that could change our spirits' DNA.

Blessing

Sunlight through the window conquers
shadows from overhanging trees.
All is in order for my friend,
for his final journey.

His breaths are strained
but beneath, peace pervades.
His goodbye is brief.
He shakes my hand.

There is a glint in his eyes
as he passes down a father's blessing
meant for the son he never had.
He speaks the simple words

'Be a good man.'

Return

Light fades with footfalls
as the blazing light rages by and a trail bike
carries the worries of a working day home.

Shining eucalypts line
the road of dusty clay
that winds between the houses and the hill.

From the highway the lantern line
of peak-hour traffic roars.
I turn and walk back towards the stillness

of the orange and gold sunset
over the corrugated Brindabellas
beneath a crescent moon.